AIFEST International Poetry Compilation
December 2020

Volume V
Open Category

Shades of Love and Shadows of Life
An Anthology of Love Poetry

All India Forum for English Students, Scholars and Trainers (AIFEST)

Shades of Love and Shadows of Life
An Anthology of Love Poetry

First Published
January 2021

Publisher
**All India Forum for English Students, Scholars and Trainers
(AIFEST)**

Amazon KDP ISBN: 9798585819377

Imprint
Independently Published

Editing and Proofreading
Manu Mangattu

About the Volume

To make optimum use of the Corona forced break from academic work, and to make learning fun, All India Forum for English Students, Scholars and Trainers (AIFEST) organized an Online International Poetry Competition for lovers of literature and poetry in November 2020. The participants were divided into three categories: Middle School (Classes V to VIII), High School (Classes IX to XII), and an Open Category for everyone else. Themes for poetry were different for different categories.

The results were announced on 20th November 2020, following which recitations of selected poems were compiled and posted on the Official YouTube Channel of AIFEST. We left no stone unturned to ensure free, fair and just evaluation and competition. We also made sure that unbiased and capable judges evaluated the poems. The relevant details were posted on the official blog and emailed to the participants. All the submissions were checked for plagiarism using both Turnitin and Urkund software.

Due to the huge volume of submissions we received, we had to omit many submissions based on the overall grade and score. We also understand that despite our best attempts, there could be subjectivity in evaluation and judgment. Pure objectivity, especially in evaluating poetry, is almost impossible. Please remember that even TS Eliot and William Wordsworth had faced rejection from reputed publishers.

From the Open Category, 252 poems were awarded A Grade. These were sorted and edited based on the subject matter, point of view, and treatment of the theme. This anthology features 78 poems on the theme 'Shades of Love' compiled for the perusal and consumption of the enthusiasts. It is also sincerely hoped that the volumes of this anthology will find their place in libraries and book houses as a periodical literary compilation documenting the output of a pandemic stricken multitude.

Poets Featuring in this Volume

1. Sandra James, Karunapuram, Idukki, Kerala
2. Aneri Gandhi, JG College Of Commerce ASIA Campus Ahmedabad
3. Nadar Joel Ebenezer Raju, St John College of Humanities and Science, Vevoor, Palghar
4. Disha Gupta, Bajrang Colony, Jhansi, UP
5. Aswani R Jeevan, Department of English, Farook College, Calicut
6. Ashmita Bora, IIIT, Guwahati, Bongora, Guwahati
7. Dr Asha Rani Anto, R H Patel B Ed College Gandhinagar, Gujarat
8. Abin Mathew, St Dominic's College, Kanjirappally Kerala
9. Praneetha, Sapthagiri Heights, Kukatpally, Hyderabad
10. Prakash Shamjibhai Chauhan, Department of English & CLS Saurashtra University
11. Anguri Hazra, St Xavier's College Burdwan
12. Savita Shastri, Surana College, Bangalore
13. Gouri H Nair, Fatima Mata National College (Autonomous), Kollam, Kerala
14. Khushi Yadav, Amity University, Gwalior Madhya Pradesh
15. Sharmila Jajodia, Ramniranjan Jhunjhunwala College Ghatkopar, Mumbai
16. Sheetal VB, Tilakwadi Belagavi, Karnataka
17. K Ruhaiya Afrin, Tirunelveli
18. Shivani Sarat, Amity University Noida
19. Vittal Navi, Govt First Grade College Mudhol, Bagalkot
20. Ronil Soni, JG Group of Colleges, Ahmedabad, Gujarat
21. Afina Reshmi C, St Jerome's College of Arts and Science Anandhanadarkudy
22. Jayeeta Paul, Women's College, Calcutta
23. Rinsa Joy, MD College, Kunnamkulam, Kerala
24. Neenu Thomas, Don Bosco Arts and Science College Angadikadav
25. Jesna Khanun, Calicut, Kerala
26. Sabarinathan V, Loyola College of Arts and Science

Mettala Namakkal
27. Reshma LR, St Cyril's College, Adoor, Kerala
28. Ananya Verma, Jagran Lakecity University Chandanpura Bhopal
29. Sundari Johnson, V G Vaze College of Arts, Science and Commerce
30. Brillya G, Pondicherry University, Kalapet, Puducherry
31. Swetha Rajkumar, Bharathidasan Govt College for Women Puducherry
32. Glory Elsa Tom, St Dominic's College, Kanjirapally Kerala
33. Syed Tamjeed Ali, Aurangabad, Maharashtra
34. P Nisha, Auxilium College (Autonomous) Vellore, Tamil Nadu
35. Tanisha Rathod, Jagran Lakecity University, Bhopal
36. Syed Saba Rizvi, Jamia Millia Islamia, New Delhi
37. Noor Mohammed Maheera, Auxilium College Vellore
38. Aishwarya Lakkakula, RBVRR Women's College Narayanguda, Hyderabad
39. Hemasreelatha M, Shri Shankarlal Sundarbai Shasun Jain College (W) Chennai
40. S Vijaya Rekha, Sarojini Naidu Vanita Maha Vidyalaya Nampally
41. Dimple Nahata, Alipore Road, Kolkata
42. Piyali Dey, Seshadripuram First Grade College Bangalore
43. Foram Rikky Shah, Shri Shankarlal Sundarbai Shasun Jain College for Women
44. Razanna Niaz, Mosque Street, Madhavalayam, Kanyakumari
45. Muskan Jain, Amity University Madhya Pradesh
46. Abhijit Seal, Cotton University, Panbazar, Guwahati Assam
47. Jyoti Kushwaha, Bundelkhand University, Jhansi
48. Khubi Ram, Aggarwal Public School, Ballabgarh
49. Rathod Hetal, Krantiguru Shyamji Krushna Verma Kachchh University, Bhuj
50. Aashi Prasad, Jyoti Nivas College, Banglore
51. Mamidi Shireesha, Andhra University, Vishakapatnam
52. Ahalya, Pandaravilai, Kandanvilai, Kanyakumari

53. Upanisha S, Avinashilingam Institute for HS & HE for Women Coimbatore
54. Vishnu Priya J, Bharathamatha College of Arts and Sciences Kozhnjampara
55. Jyotsana, Mata Sundari College for Women, Delhi
56. Mickey Manaswini, Balugaon, Khordha
57. Dhanashree Das, Indira Gandhi National Open University, Guwahati
58. Anagha Agnes, Pondicherry University
59. Sooraj Lal SB, Tattamangalam, Palakkad
60. Achudha S, St Joseph's College of Arts and Science Cuddalore, Tamil Nadu
61. Rachit Dave, Odhav Avenue, Pramukhswami Nagar Bhuj
62. D Ruban Prabu, Kovilpatti, Thoothukudi
63. CS Ashitha Hanna, East Peruvilai, Nagercoil
64. Prakruti Vinayak Naik, Om Sai Dham, Davangere
65. Ayesha Rahman, Lucknow
66. Tanya Tripathi, IFHE, Donthanpalle, Telangana
67. Bishal Bimal Mazumdar, Nalbari College, Nalbari Assam
68. Tabinda Naiyer, Bardhaman
69. Tayyaba Barqi, Amity University Dubai
70. Nandhini A, Lady Doak College, Madurai
71. Atiendriya Verma, VIT University, Bhopal, Madhya Pradesh
72. Surya Ratna Sarvani Addanki, Dr SR Arts College Visakhapatnam
73. Lorna Barbara Erla, Jagran Lakecity University Mugaliyachap, Bhopal (MP)
74. S Nandhini, The American College, Madurai
75. Shruti Ganesh, National Institute of Design, Ahmedabad
76. Garima Nandal, Sonipat, Haryana
77. Abdu Rahiman M, Kolathur, Malappuram, Kerala
78. Niteesh KR, Nagasandra, Bangalore

1
Shape of Shadow
Sandra James, Karunapuram, Idukki, Kerala

It was half past midnight
Flies were fluttering around the street light.

I saw a shadow as frightening as a skeleton
Over the theatre wall.

My limbs were pulled away
And I fell in the clay.

IT crawled towards me
Beneath the Gulmohar.

I searched for my specs;
It was lying next to some broken branches.

Placing it on the curves of my nose
I mounted the woods and crossed it.

My shadow got vanquished by that of the shanty town
Erected behind me; Looking Forward!

As the figure rolled up its shadow
Got revealed under the light.

A fragile one debilitated by penury
Stood in front of me.

My feet moved along with that shadow
To find uncountable ones out there in the streets.
A soft groan was heard behind the tin sheets.
A humped one walked towards us with much difficulty.

Another little one whose balloon-like belly walking ahead it
Crawled out of a concrete pipe that lined a sprawling division.

Within the blinking of my eyes, I found a huge cluster of
Shadows grew around me.

Suddenly, an eagle hooked me
With its lethal nails up to the orb of night.

I saw my shadow there in the lane getting melded with the
cluster
Forming the Shape of Heart.

Street lamps shed light over it
And the lighted love was beating.

2
It's That Word

Aneri Gandhi, JG College Of Commerce ASIA Campus
Ahmedabad

It comes in many shades,
But the feeling is one.

It comes in many forms,
But the connection is one.

It is beautiful,
But complicated.

It is natural,
But different for everyone.

It is inside me and everyone else,
But everyone feels it differently.

It is very strong,
But it melts down easily.

It is enough powerful,
But is misunderstood.

It could save the human inside us,
It could save the planet earth,
It could save the species that coexist with us,
It could give humanity a better future.

It's just the way we see it,
It's one of the most powerful quality.

It's one thing on which most of philosophically beautiful things
are written.
I also wanted to make contribution to that philosophies,
But then thought let's keep it to me.

If it works,
It would be evident.

If it won't,
I will let you know.

It's that word with four letters,
You know that right?

3
The Story of Love
Nadar Joel Ebenezer Raju, St John College of Humanities and
Science, Vevoor, Palghar

Love; it's an amazing feeling
It's never a coincidence to anyone
Life is incomplete without having it.
Love exist everywhere.

Love is like a flowing breeze,
it was never for only one.
Love is so amazing that even small things can be the reason to
win your hearts.

Love has seen everything.
Love knows everything.
It knows when it should come in your life.
Love doesn't have castes or favouritism.

The first taste of love, is a mother.
Through whom we came to know that,
Love has no boundaries.

Love came in our life as a form of God.
God helped us to know that,
God's love was unconditional.
God gave the same love to humans.

Loving became humans major trait.
We saw everything, everyone through the eyes of love.
This is how love was kind, it wasn't arrogant.
Love started to evolve in us. Slowly and steadily love started to
hurt people.
Humans used love as a weapon.
Love resulted in violence.
Love resulted in wars.

Love and war?

Never made sense
But that what happened.
Wars shed innocent blood
Love broke itself before us humans.

Everywhere you see,
was lust, pride, hatred, envy, blasphemy.
There was no love found on humans from that day.
This really broke God's heart...

Then there was new dawn.
When some humans turned on.
They used their hearts instead of brains.
Kindness became a key and changed the world.

Love started to glow.
Through that seed of kindness
Love started to evolve again.
And this time humans kept it.
Love started to glow everywhere.
Pride started to perish.
Lust started to wither.
World started to heal.
And at the end
They was so much love in the world that God said to himself,
"Heaven I'm in heaven, Earth is the new Heaven."

4
A Dream of Togetherness
Disha Gupta, Bajrang Colony, Jhansi, UP

Woven a dream of togetherness,
And a silent promise of forgiveness.
Without saying who is right or wrong,
We will sing the same song.

How you came to my life,
Looking at your picture on your profile,
I admired your silence and sincerity,
It made me feel we are united, till infinity.

The first time I heard your voice,
How my heart pounced and I rejoiced.
From a clan of warrior and man of swords,
How to describe you in few words

On the waters, your ship sails
Here, I wait in the reply of your mails.
For the world calls you a sailor,
You are no less than an epitome of valour.

From the gentle to violent wave,
Restless for your love I crave.
Busy with your trade and war,
I admire you looking at the star.

Battling with the storms of sea,
And breaking all the norms of breeze,
Tossing the anchor and rolling the rudder,
You came winning out of every hurdle.

Long time later you came,
And make our love tale gain some fame,
Spread everywhere the symbol of dove,
Paint me in the colour of love.

Our love is huge and Icelandic
A silent oath and commitment on Titanic
Offering me, heart of ocean and ring,
There, I pronounce you as my King.

5
On Lofty Love
Aswani R Jeevan, Department of English, Farook College
Calicut

The loft

Inside,
Near the footboard
My books, bemused…
In the hanger
His military uniform;
With countable medals…
On the three-legged table
My pen… his gun…
On the wooden plank
My scarf… his hat…
In the cushioned chair
Our belts, boldly entangled.

Out,
At the doorstep
Our black-eyed puppy…
A broken sandal, unseen and
A new pair of branded boots
A desiccated water-well with
Four bloomed cactus plants

On the road,
A bus that misses the time
Three or four chatty women
A box store… One in debt
And,
The high noon beams of summer

Inside,
Pain
Sweat
Bitter

Laughter

Out,
Pain
Sweat
Bitter
Laughter

OUTSIDE IN
INSIDE OUT

Done!
We were conjugating!

(I am reciting the uniform
He is putting on the books

Now, you go back Mr Peeper!
Take the broken sandal back
If it has your name gravely engraved)

6
Nothing beyond You
Ashmita Bora, IIIT, Guwahati, Bongora, Guwahati

The dews on the leaves glistened like pearls in the morning light,
The rose buds played peek-a-boo amongst the swaying bush.
Her lacy nightgown brushed across the moist grass of the lawn,
Her warm hands caressed the petals of the blooming marigolds,
The morning sun seemed to herald her in all its glory.

He sat on a cane chair in the veranda,
A cup of tea in front of him,
His eyes transfixed on her.
If only he could have given her what her heart desired,
A child... a child to call their own.
He knew he was incapable of that,
And it was killing him alive.
Motherhood beckoned her,
A woman's greatest joy!
All he wanted to give her was a child,
A child to dote over and adore,
To fulfil her heart's longings and more.
How he loved her, he wished he could say,
To make her the happiest wife, so her heart would sway.
But finally, he had decided, he had to let her go.
She will someday find bliss with someone better, he knew.

She fondled the flawlessly white lilies,
Their perfume filled up the air.
The strong scent made something come alive within her.
The cold dew tingled her bare feet,
Her entirety felt alive to the core.
She could feel his eyes on her,
She could sense his guilt, his misery, his helplessness.
She pretended not to see.
A moment of epiphany.
It dawned on her now,
He was the love of her life.
She could never want anything more.

For him even her being's utmost desire,
She knew she could forego.

7
Flavours of Love

Dr Asha Rani Anto, RH Patel B Ed College, Gandhinagar
Gujarat

Love that is not fragile and whimsical all the time
Just to ponder the shades of love is the love which is perennial
and divine.

That's where the mother's love is, all cervical and keeps up the
adrenaline
A mother's love is a superb love bundled from paradise with
exceptional consideration.
Up and above the sky limitless, shades of love from mother
without any juxtaposition
A mother's affection resembles no other love that you can look
at.
A mother's adoration is refined by blessed messengers and
streams legitimately from her spirit.

Shades of love that's most regardful and graced upon
He is the father whom you model on
He never hooks for compliments.
He's never one to cater wrong supplements.
He just goes on toiling with his life, grinding and grilling in hard
weather
For those he loves the most. Not to thither but be together
Tumultuous at time but protector all the time

Brother and sister complements of life, their shade of love is
invisible but infinite
They may fight and frown
But they do because they feel we are their own
In happiness and agony, they stand by and cuddle us so not to
worry

Shades of love that is like fresh air may be platonic, may be
crush or romantic at time
Lover, spouse and sweetheart all together in one rhyme

Love's labour may be lost, but it is something to boast
Towards the evening when we hold together shades of love
become luminescent, found and lost.
Such is the shade of love who loves you without making another
shade out of you

Curious, quirky, happy and sad all the while
It's our children, who make our life merry and agile.
Innocent and ignorant at times, that is the shade of love which is
serene yet chaotic
Because this shade of love is eternal and biotic

Love of friend is like the finest gem hard to find
This shade of love is needed all the time and bring the little
shine.
Understanding all your shades of love, bring camaraderie in your
life
Shade of love without your friends is broken arrow nowhere
Here, there and everywhere doth somewhere.

When it's all said, what to hope for in the shades of love
Is the love for divine, numb and naive at a blow?
Omnipotent & omnipresent
To feel the essence, look up the sky saying you are now to
descend
That's shade of love is hard to find as it's there always in you.

All shades of love is having multicoloured dimensions
Some are pure, some are faithful, some bring happiness and
some bring connections.
Life is full of love when all the shades are intact forever
But it's me who is the artist and can put all the shades of love all
together.
Make my painting of 'life', a masterpiece
And be my own love that's the peace
Shades of love in relation are varied, so gather each piece.

8
Colours of Love
Abin Mathew, St Dominic's College, Kanjirappally, Kerala

Love has many shades,
Some shades we see are not the shade of love

Love has many shades,
But don't be a colour blind in selecting the perfect shade

Love has many shades,
But sometimes you may not be able to recognise the colour of
some shades

I love the shade of love,
That I see in my father's face, It brightens like the morning sun,
that brights for others

I love the shade of love,
That I see in my mother's face at the end of the day, it is black in
colour due to her works.

I love the shade of love,
Which came like a teardrop from my parents eyes when I gave
them my first salary

Throughout out my life,
I've seen many shades of love but they didn't give the colours
that I have seen in my parents.

9
There is Love in Everyone
Praneetha, Sapthagiri Heights, Kukatpally, Hyderabad

There is love of a fan
that can neither be acknowledged nor confessed
There is love of an artist
which can be seen in the art which he carved from his heart
There is love of a mother
as pure as a baby's smile which can neither be replaced nor
explained
There is love of a father
which can be seen in his effort of making the world a
comfortable place for his child to live in
There is love of a brother
which can be felt in his care and responsibility towards his
siblings.
There is love of a spouse
when they say "I Trust You" holding your hand
And then there is love of a friend
when he stands by you in your failures and celebrates your
success more than you
There is love everywhere and the one who experiences all the
shades of love is truly blessed.

10
Elope

Prakash Shamjibhai Chauhan, Department of English & CLS
Saurashtra University

I Want to Elope with you
In the beauty of darkness and
Love your unselfish love

I Want to Elope with you
In the promises of our lives and
In the Calm and warmness of uncertain love,

I want to Elope with you
In the Monsoon days of love
In the downpour drops of your love,

I want to Elope with you
In the Spring of your love
In the sweet kisses of your springy lips,

I want elope with you
In the heart stopping winter
In the tender and comfortable hugs of your body

I want to elope with you like Romeo
In the mid night vacant street of our city
In the sexy midnight night of Verona

I want to elope with you like Wickham
In the Jane Austen's Pride and Prejudice
In the chapters number 46 to 49

I want to elope with you
In the lovely and innocent face of your
In the on your chick

I want to elope with you
In the white beauty of your skin

In the Sweet tangy melodious singing

I Want to Elope with you
In the Sober and Lovely Personality of your
In Neither Miranda, Claudia, Gertrude, Lady Macbeth nor by
Desdemona, Cleopatra

I want to Elope with you
In the heart beat of our heart
In the veins of our blood

I want to Elope with you as Jack Dowson
In the bifurcation of Titanic gigantic ship
In the hug and hold of Rose Dewitt Bukater

Honey! Let's Elope with us together
In the soul of each other
In the shape of heart made by our hands

11
Broken but Beautiful
Anguri Hazra, St Xavier's College Burdwan

What if memories don't heal the broken parts
But make us hold on stronger
Hurting more each day?
What if 'unfollowing' is no longer an option??
Will you be get over then!
To be honest, it is never over
Never over still we both stay
We will tend to be each other's last option
Till time stops to slither away.

12
Love: A Magical Word
Savita Shastri, Surana College, Bangalore

'Love', a word with just four letters, whose meaning transcends
all depths;
An amalgamation of pleasure and pain, an emotion that brings
you loss and gain;
An expression that crosses all boundaries, a feeling that is
wrapped in mysteries;
A trail which has its ups and downs, an emotional blend of
smiles and frowns;
A feeling that defies age and gender, a sentiment that is so pure
and tender;
Love makes you a better person, a sensation that thrills you all
season;
The way you feel when you meet your soul mate is Love;
The way you feel when your toddler takes the first step is Love;
The way you feel when your little one makes it big in life is
Love;
The way you feel when your big brother promises to take care of
you is Love;
The way you feel when your kid sister turns a mom is Love;
The way you feel when you see your elderly parents healthy is
Love,
The way you feel when your pets come clinging on to you is
Love;
The way you feel when you wake up to the chirping of birds is
Love;
The way you feel when the Tricolour rises above all is Love;
The feeling of joy when you see your loved ones smile is Love;
The feeling of helplessness seeing your loved ones in pain is also
Love;
Love makes life a worthy experience, Life without love gives a
feeling of absence;
Living for each other, living with each other is Love;
Staying away from each other, with a desire to unite with each
other is Love;

Love, a simple four letter magical word, stories of which
everyone has heard;
Giggles, kisses, hugs, heartaches, fights, break-ups, patch-ups,
all part of Love;
'Love', a word with just four letters, whose meaning transcends
all depths.

13
The Shades of Love
Gouri H Nair, Fatima Mata National College (Autonomous),
Kollam, Kerala

My flowering stage has witnessed
The hopes and dreams of love
Which craves the soul of passion
That carves the path of satisfaction

I beg, I cried, and I crave
To see the love in life
Which I longed a lover in the way
Unluckily detached away

I am blind to see the colours
Those colours of love
Which lacks in my soul
That frozen me whole

Now I can see those bright colours
In that, I can see my soul clearer
Which I dig it from the lord nature
The guardian of the whole universe

I am aware about those different shades
From the lessons taught from my mother earth
Who showers the wisdom upon me
That makes my vision more clear

As we can see the different colours
Dispersed by a water droplet by the showering of sun
I could be able to see the shades of love
The wisdom only acquired by his fondling of love

14
Shades of Love
Khushi Yadav, Amity University, Gwalior, Madhya Pradesh

A perpetual silence all around,
All I could hear was my soul's sound
Our memories upheaving in my head,
Evacuating these memories which were never dead.
"Years were passing with you & you stayed as near & dear like a
beautiful present"

The night we met was a random one,
It may have been so long ago, but still like you I've met none
We were just 20' when you looked at me for the first juncture,
& since that night every meeting with you was a rapture.
"Sceptically & credibly my golden heart was blooming the
flowers of love"

At 23' you were the solution to all my gloomy feelin',
But still to stay together with we were dealin'
Together we were exploring the 'shades of our love'
With every misunderstandings & understandings our love was
raising above.
"It was good to be loved, but we profound to understand each
other"

We were of 25' when you asked for hand my hand,
And the happy, sad moments with you were passing like sand
Every shade with your was perfect like a full moon night,
You completed me like a perfectly bloomed mallow.
"Scrabbling together we were completing our story with all these
shades of our love"

15
Technology, Art and Love

Sharmila Jajodia, Ramniranjan Jhunjhunwala College
Ghatkopar, Mumbai

Love is life in the age of technology.
Love is life in the age and page of art.
Love is life in the mind of lovers
Whichever age they belong to.
Love is ageless, timeless and space less.
It flourishes in the imagination of lovers
With the help of technology and art
Whichever age they belong to.
Love knows no barriers
of caste, class, creed, religion and nation.
It knows only one language i.e., humanism
Whichever age they belong to.
Technology has made love easier and simpler,
Lovers can connect to each other hassle free
anytime from anywhere.
Art too plays a prominent role
as pure love is always artistic, simplistic,
and non-abusive.
No technology, no art is misused
Whichever age they belong to.
Only feelings are used
To express feelings of love
Through technology and art,
And love is made for love's sake
No selfish motives are ingrained.
They live love, love lovely feelings
Because they love each other
Whichever age they belong to.
They don't dupe each other before or after union.
They don't meet each other for lust and hunger.
They don't ditch each other for materialistic gains,
Whichever age they belong to.
They don't splash acid on each other
to force love on each other.

They don't try to test love
by making illogical demands
Which make the other permanently Handicap,
Whichever age they belong to.
True love gives the other equal space.
It doesn't expect the other to be a slave.
It treats the other as a human being
Full of emotions,
Not a commodity to consume,
Whichever age they belong to.
True love doesn't suspect the other.
It is not a relation for convenience and compromise.
It is a bond of understanding,
Whichever age they belong to.
Love is blind, half-blind, true-false or pure-impure
A temporary contract, or a permanent relation?,
Is not defined by social or cultural norms
But by the intentions of the Lovers,
Whichever age they belong to.
Love doesn't Tweet love,
Love doesn't post Whats App chats,
Love doesn't gets viral on social networking sites,
Love doesn't share photographs on Facebook.
It just realizes itself in the inner room of the two selves.

16
Shades of Love
Sheetal VB, Tilakwadi Belagavi, Karnataka

I have loved u, more than love itself,
I have understood u, more than love itself, but
This fact either I know or my heart does.
Come my dear love, come and accept everything of mine as
yours.
Come and accept the relationship of my love
I can be anything for you, but you are that someone special for
whom I breadth.
The moment you come close to me, my heart skips a beat, the
rhythm of my heart beat changes.
The aroma of your existence, brushes my body as the wind
blows
The fire of love that you have lit within me, makes me burn in
the fire of your dreams.
I'm worried to know the result of my exam called "love"
How should I tell you, how scared I'm for the truth that your
love may take my life away….

17
Besotted in Love
K Ruhaiya Afrin, Tirunelveli

Spring gives me a reason to smile at you.
This beautiful weather has destroyed me.
God created you with shades of beauty.
You gaze me with shades of love.
You are hidden in my shades of dream.
You shattered my loniless with shades of affection.
You are the shadow of my feelings.
You will be immortal in my thoughts.
Your charm makes me warm.
The heat of your memories make my moments melt.
You have shades over me.
When I surrounded by you,
It exudes the sweet aroma like cherries in March.
Colour me in the colour of love.
Neither you nor I cannot escape from the adventure of love.
Can lighthouse shows the way to reach you?.

18
Shades of Lilac
Shivani Sarat, Amity University Noida

10.14 PM
My vision blurs,
I spell colours of doom, out on my skins,
While melancholically tracing them scars, I fight
I come upon an engulfing one, gift of the war.
On the right cheek below my blue eyes,
First robust, then a bright maroon.
The only one harmless in there now,
Were his deep lilac shadows
Shallow than his thoughtless mind.
Were these the shades of love?

11.20 PM
The scars evolve, now bluish black,
My body, a palette, he leaves me in a slack,
Hearing the door whisper, my insides crack,
First his shadows, then him. Doom was my fate.
Tangled nerves. Anticipating heart. Perspiring, I wait.
Oh! Burn down those flickering eyes, they hurt.
My shadow, perfect as ever, hiding the coloured scars.
Unbiased and upturning
She was my lilac reflection.
Were these the shades of love?

12.40 AM
My lips sealed and stitched.
The screams die down in my parched throat.
Emancipating a sound from my navel, unheard by all.
Stripped of my sanity and ripped off my soul.
A twisted ankle and a bruised chin,
Colourless mind with a flawed body.
My shadow remains the same as 11.20.
The wounds fresh and dripping.
Stinking off unfulfilled promises, he smirks.
Neighbours and surrounding oblivious, I sleep.

It's okay. You don't apologize for your survival.
Lilac shadows cast on me, in darkness.
Was this abuse the shades of love?

1.30 AM
Of sensations and emotions
mumbling away in silence
were rusted spirits
of pain and love.

Violet for the flowers
that decorated my crib in childhood
Indigo for the ink
that sprawled over my uniform in middle school
Blue for the colour of the bright sky
when we stole our first glance
Green for the lush meadow
I drew whilst I was in kindergarten
Yellow for Ma's saree
which papa and I gifted her last year
Orange for the ice lolly
I had in the most humid summers of 2016
And finally, Red for the colour of our love
and the roses we picked
on our first date.

Do you recollect the pink?
and the maroon and white?
the bright lime green?
Were these the forgotten shades?

02.10 AM
Clothes in shreds, I now dread.
Destructive is it, to find a home, dead.
To find a home, in a heartbeat, in a person, whom I used.
My ankle swollen, evident from my shadows.
Lay I now bland, retracting the new scars so bright.
Shackled to a heartbeat, abuse, my meal, I hope 12.40 dies.
The cigarette puff reminds me of my heartbeak, my first one.

The hell within awakes stripping my soul, of its sanity.
Again, I sigh loud as he leaves, with his shadow, so dirty.
Innocence lost in the face of my lilac past
My past emerges with my shadows.
Shadows so bad that they fade.

03.08 AM
My gaze falters,
Shadows to live to move, halts.
Wind above, scenting of reeked lips.
Auburn hair over my scars, I force myself.
I force myself to run through the street of memories.
Through the dingy streets of guilt and pain, shadows along.
With those scars, embrace yourself.
Be an art, a masterpiece. Let the dreams rise as the Sun.
Bruised body with a discoloured skin, violet, black, blue,
maroon.
Never hope it returns, my lilac heartbeat.
The nights of horror and days of contour less sunrises.
Mysterious shadows engulf your blemishes.
Keep retracting scars to remind them of those pasts.

A million strangers
and familiar faces
toenails struck on threads
grasping together
a million promises
A dark street
and a few deep alleys
Used polaroids
in shadows of twilight
and dances in the rain
loneliness thriving in lust
Your light brown eyes
Pierce into mine
snowflakes on oak
your criminal lips curve
Asking a question
"Are these the shades of love?"

19
True Love
Vittal Navi, Govt First Grade College Mudhol, Bagalkot

Love is like a little fragrance, not me
But come with me to catch that
If it had flown, don't worry!
I will pour and pour

Bouquet has many flowers, not me
I have only you, sometimes slipped!
Don't hate me and left me.
I will love you, I still love you

Someone dislikes you, not me
I still have a large hands for you
If your hearts bell is rings me
I will there! I still there!

20
One Strange Evening
Ronil Soni, JG Group of Colleges, Ahmedabad, Gujarat

One strange evening reminds me of something beautifully
known,
It could be only our love.

It makes me want to repeat our story again,
It makes me want to feel the story of us again,

I love different colours of Sun,
Which reminds me our shades of love.

In the Blue sky the Yellow colour of Sun is attracting me
towards the evening,
Just as how i was attracted by you.

The way Orange evolve in Yellow,
It looks like we were evolved in each other.

The stroke of Red is filled in my heart as our selfless and
unconditional love,
The shades of sky are just different as our shades of love.

Though you are not with me, Your love is always with me.

21
His Mrs
Afina Reshmi C, St Jerome's College of Arts and Science
Kanyakumari, Tamil Nadu

(Are you a good reader? then feel the Aura hiding in every line)
She is a pretty young girl
Sitting aside of me...!
Sh! She is mocking at me
The look through her specs was marvellous
Rarely she does but I'm interested to go on...!
Her tiny lips were coloured by raspberries
Flavour of the fragrance tempt me to go closer
With silence – My heart says
Formerly goodness brings you here
I'm falling again and again inside – The ditch
Twinkles in her cheeks (O! Not by seeing me
But the fiction in her hands)
I forbid myself, Yet I can't
I think, I've lost All mine in her
The cool breeze made a melody
With the giant fear – I
Knelt down front to her feet
The horrifying face over me turns blushing
With the pathetic smile, She surrendered herself to me
Possibly we were married
Days, Months, and Years rolled by...!
With Grey hair and wrinkled face we are
Everything was filled with changes
Even I'm left alone, after her separation
I'm sure, She must lean out of the window of paradise
Just looking for her care
I don't want to give her strain, so I'm near to her hands now...!
We were not dead, still we are alive beyond the word Love
She is the world's best wife
Yes, She is my beloved Mrs.

22
Contrast of Love
Jayeeta Paul, Women's College, Calcutta

The nature gives love to us,
In return expect nothing.
The mother gives birth to us,
To give us the caring.

If you had the eyes
To seek the beauty of cosmos;
You can feel the love is eternal
Not bounded by material.

This creation never be survived,
If the One has never shown the love.
Not we have been here
To cherish the beauty of earth.

Love is not bound in physicality,
Not in charms.
Love is the sunshine of eternal flame
That cannot be measured.

So who are we,
To judge the fragments of love?
We are just some sparks,
The evidence of eternal warmth.

We create riots and wars,
Make humans create the scars;
But nature never forget to heal,
Not forget to bloom a flower in spring.

Some men tried to pull the trigger;
Some to cherish the blood
Some for love of land,
This is also love, we never disagree to that.

The sun is setting, the glow has gone.
It's time to reunite with family one
Alas! The predator have to prey
To feed the mouth of little one.

At the end of day some loves grow
Some fallen apart with the flow.
The shades are different, meaning is huge.
This four letter word,
Makes a different world for you.

23
She
Rinsa Joy, MD College, Kunnamkulam, Kerala

Calmness in her eyes, drought in her lips
That shiny golden hair smells odd,
Wrinkles in her cheek shows her countless days,
Her pleasant attitude-the warmth of her family,
The mighty hands made everything humble,
The 7th hand build the alter of her brood,
Her strong desires magically resembling her beauty.

The hours make her afraid,
Every day and night she feels exquisite pain
The pain of solace, console, affection …
Her strength, her brood, all are fading
She kneels to pray for see her destiny
Her candles are melting,
Her veil of grace blurred by whispers…

Her quest for love was a deep hallow, hallow of darkness
She is digging for love. At length,
She finds a mere shadow,
A mere shadow of her ménage,
That fathomed ménage –
Gave her their warmth, their tenderness, their fondness…
By and by she gains her shadow of love and her veil of grace.

24
Forbidden!
Neenu Thomas, Don Bosco Arts and Science College
Angadikadav, Kerala

I woke by knitting the crumbled
Ashes from smokey pyre!
I peeped in for candlelit marches,
To lighten a path for the cursed
'Awaara', dumped mercilessly.
None came to apply turpentine
Drops over the oozing pores of
Lusty vengeance; indeed forbidden!

I walked, caressing the fragile leaf
Strands of pearl millets; reckoning
Extremes of grief in mind,
Witnessing the silence of the downtrodden.
Futile life and cemetery of my
Impure body.
I chiseled my deep wounds with
The same sickle I did the last harvest.

I glanced at the meek cows feeding
Upon the fodder smudged with
My vaginal blood; thence nauseating,
Myself a sinner, filtered in
The grey shades of purgatory.
I felt mesmerized by his love
Drenching in depths of affection,
Rather forgetting hierarchies.

It's FORBIDDEN!
The saffron chords of ancestral
Pedigree in royal blood shan't
Culminate in the impure love.
Then akin Jews and Blacks
Nevertheless, be cautious for
Death sentence brutally at the

Heart of many Hathras'...

I couldn't hear hailstorms
Yearning for justice,
I couldn't hear the cries of
Those great souls who could
Tear my flesh and drink
The nastily luscious untouchable blood
Dissecting my nipples and
Ripping the last sword-my tongue!

Flashlights went on hookups
With the authoritarians
Making my soul perspire
Even in the deadly cold state of being!.
Silently digesting that I'm another
Statue built akin KHAIRLANJI!.
Still, the forbidden citizens cry.
Landlords explore the thatched roofs
Of 'touchable pleasure objects'
To quench elite chauvinistic thrust!
I roared in the highest decibel
The whole of Aligarh slept early!
It's forbidden to hear weak cries.

25
Art of Love
Jesna Khanun, Calicut, Kerala

Amidst all the chaos across the globe,
It is an art of love to smile
And unfurl it to the length and breadth.
Rise from the ashes, and bring the hope.

To please them with sweetest of your words
And to fuel them with hope and dreams.
A sign of humanity to feed the un-fed, though
It is an art of love to feed their soul with love and care.

May all our children learn to dance in the rain
And the art of empathy;
To see humanity beyond borders,
rivers and cultures.

And may you see endless colorful dreams
For not to forget to love yourself.
And never leave your dreams unchased;
Till your wings fly above the clouds.

And my words of love for you,
Be a wave, rain and fire!

26
The Love Shade of Damsel and Rain

Sabarinathan V, Loyola College of Arts and Science
Mettala Namakkal

Peacock announces the arrival of rain,
Damsel brings rain on scorching desert.
On par with showering rain and silky wind,
She appears like a Queen's promenade,
Her steps disturb not, single bug beneath.

Greenish garden, Bush and groves,
Turns reddish, glow not of the sun,
But they bashful of damsel, thus blush
Drops that fell on her adored body attain
Its objectives and reason for the birth.

The untouched cry more to be born again;
The cycle of rain is all in hope of same.
The unfortunate one is that fell far,
Dark clouds contrasted her swan white-
Skin, shine like silver and platinum ring.

Skilled goldsmith nay seen such material.
They can make endless Jewel out of her-
Fallen nail bit. Completely uncontaminated.
Lightning, Thunder more of in celebration,
The rain follows wherever she goes.

There at a distance penetrating dim,
I sat on bench brooding- My eyes on her feet
The path made of thousand red rose carpet
I cut Rose petals, and the sharp thorns
It pierce and bleeds my hand, but still smiles
At seeing damsel ambulate.

Oh! My dear mistress, of highest noble heir.
Entrusted with elegant virtues;
Oh! My amiable lady, your highness incomparable.

Compassion is exquisite- that behold.

Lovely lady of laudable outlook;
Worthy goddess of dexterous deed.
Not just she follows it all above,
Indoctrinate her surroundings too.
Her tongue enunciate ill of none,
And her manner is never discourteous.

Utterance from mouth like gold dust.
But accurate exhibit womanly wisdom.
Single glance is ample of her Ken.
Her unpretentiousness is admirable
Exemplary and a book of reference
To all the women on Earth!!!

27
Love Today
Reshma LR, St Cyril's College, Adoor, Kerala

In search of 'love',
I saw you 'lust';
Who hides the true face
Of love and life,
Who deceived the mankind,
With the pompous dreams...
And you are the monster,
Who spit acid on face.
And you are the devil,
Who killed marital knots.
And you are the giant,
Who deflowered buds.
And you are the one,
Who evacuated love.

28
My Everlasting Treasures
Ananya Verma, Jagran Lakecity University, Chandanpura
Bhopal

From being born
To being loved,
I faced the phase,
Of pure parent love.

When I was young,
I was robbed of some,
When my pillar parent,
Slept in depth.

His body was cold,
And pale as a snowflake,
But his face was as beautiful,
Just as if.

The trauma shook me,
To ever love again,
But there it was,
The adolescent charmaine.

I loved and hurt,
And hurt and loved,
But I don't think,
It was ever enough.
Some shades are known,
Some shades unknown,
I fell in love,
With my own day dream.

He was perfect,
As he could be,
With curly lashes,
And a great physique.

He was the shade,
That was unknown,
Still the one,
Who was too known.

I fell so deep,
And deep in love,
Till then I knew,
He was the last shade of love.

29
Peacock Plume

Sundari Johnson, VG Vaze College of Arts, Science &
Commerce

If I, like a plume plucked from the breast of a peacock,
Be adorned on the crown of Lord Krishna,
Would you stop to stroke the hues of greens and blues,
Gently fluttering in the breeze, nodding at you on a calm, Vishu
day?
Would you care to pause; pull me out,
Bury me in the crest of your heart?
Or carry me prest between the leaves of 100 Love Sonnets of
Pablo Neruda,
Read me, savour me when lonely, at leisure,
Slowly caress your cheek with me and be mesmerized in the
softness of my touch?

30
Shades of Love
Brillya G, Pondicherry University, Kalapet, Puducherry

White, he was clad in
For White, she was clad with.
Eight and twenty years of enjambment
Had found a new end.
Umpteen colours turned dolorous;
Bright White into fright Black;
Love to loathe.
LOVE.
Snowy White was it
when they gave it to him.
They who gave all - all that they had,
Enwrapped in rage and covered with teardrop.
Creamy White was it
when he got it from them.
They who shared physical shoulders and mental shudders,
making fun of and mocking off.
Smokey White was it
when he shared it with him.
He who said: give it to your enemies too,
For I am it and I spare it.
Silvery White was it when he found her
She who he wanted to share his nuptial bed with.
Dimgrey was it when it was unrequited;
Davysgrey it turned when his heels were kicked;
Charcol it became when he was scorned;
Angelic Black it evolved when
"self" was born and "Love" was gone.
'Little bead of selfish Black
belittles the celestial selfless White',
All shades of Love decisively dissolved
In the pellucid liquid he held---- His Black nefarious hands made
her White face amorphous.
Heavenly love in bride and groom White
camouflaged into deadly dried and gloomy Night.
Now, dead she was and laid in a freezer bed,

And almost dead he in a dark prison cell.
Filthy white he was clad in
for white shroud she was clad with.-----
The Black and White extremes of
LOVE.

31
Call me by Love
Swetha Rajkumar, Bharathidasan Govt College for Women
Puducherry

Autumn breezes, coffee brews and gazing out of a cold pane of a
dainty little café
I can see love walking hand in hand whilst waiting for winter to
come,
To bundle up and warm their loved ones, to snuggle in life and
happiness.
Across the room, I can see a mother coddle her baby while her
son laughs in merry at her antics,
Two elderly women with crinkled smiles as warm as the evening
sun; giggle in the corner like teens holding hands while they
converse,
I can hear dogs barking and pulling at their leash to run around
fallen leaves,
Just like children circling around their weary parents in glee,
How different is one from another when Love is everywhere?

They say love is blind; but I see love in shades,
Sometimes a bit too intense,
Like the red bruises that one adorns because love is hard,
Sometimes mellow,
Like the laughter yellow on the new wedded couples lips,
A bit too dark at times,
For sometimes love is birthed through beautiful pain
A bit too bleak other times,
For love is innocent, pure and everything that's shy to be painted
in hate.

Love is universal,
Love is alien,
For there's no definite love, no perfect love and sometimes, no
love is love,
Then why is Love being measured?
You and I,

How different is our love if all we give and live by is made of
this and nothing else?
Why then should Love be labelled?
For the shade of Love one mortal loves another in, is the shade
of their soul being as One.

32
Symphony of Love
Glory Elsa Tom, St Dominic's College, Kanjirapally, Kerala

The sparkling blue blankets
Gently caressed my toes
The melody of Zephyr
Kissed my skin
My lips turned upward
Feeling the nourishing love of nature.

How to define love?
My mind posed for a while
But, never came an answer
Except some cherished memories.

Once, sitting in a park
My eyes sparkled with joy
Gazing at an old couple
Laughing together,
Cherishing the memories.
Then, my heart uttered
Love is eternal.

Sitting in the balcony,
adorning the beauty of eventide
My eyes drifted down
The little one giggling in her mother's lap
Getting squeezed in her love.
My heart uttered
Love is tender.

Walking through the busy street
My legs ceased at that sight
A young boy
Offering his hand to the blind man.
My heart remarked
Love is care.

Waiting at the traffic
I saw a stirring scene
The waiter at the shop
Running behind the stranger
To return his left out wallet.
My heart rejoiced
Love is kind.

Tapping on the handrest
My heart thumbed loudly
The fear of first flight!
But, a soft touch calmed me
And my lips flashed a smile
The smile of gratitude.
My heart whispered
Love is trust.

Love is like a rainbow
with multiple hues.

33
Two-Shadows
Syed Tamjeed Ali, Aurangabad, Maharashtra

In daylight dark,
A shadow creeps,
In the darkest of dark,
A shadow tugs me, shrugs me,
Resting my face on her shoulder,
Me a ship without rudder,
Two shadows fall into actuality,
Two shadows scream.

Due dialogues 'n remarks,
Flowing persuasions 'n sparks,
Perceptions turn dark crème,
Two shadows fall into disparity,
Two shadows scream.

Turbulence 'n yearning embarks,
Eagerness never disembarks,
Ease on each to gratify,
Two eyes fall into similarity,
Two shadows scream.

34
Shade of Love

P Nisha, Auxilium College (Autonomous) Vellore, Tamil Nadu

Love is versatile pleasure
Make us care and cherish
Really like nostalgic
Addicted to sentiments
Of emotion
Shades of love express tenderness of silence
which bloom to hold experience
To feel affection
To grow successful
Shades of love makes us to
Thrive in...

35
Shades of Love
Tanisha Rathod, Jagran Lakecity University, Bhopal

Love is blind, love is divine
It makes our soul pure and kind

Love is never seen by our eyes,
But always felt by our hearts.

Love is in that beautiful feeling,
When baby kicks in mother's belly and she is just smiling

Love is immortal, there will be no total (Calculative)
It is the feeling, Where there is no bargaining.

Love is not a bond to bind,
It provides us sky for flying.

Love is not always meant to show
But it demands to grow

Love is in bickering of couples,
It is in their jealousy and anger for each other.

Love is in tears, if it is for our dears
Love is in pain, if it helps to make someone something gain.

Love is not only relationship between Men and Women
Love is about connections.
Whether It is thing or our heart, animal or we human
Whether It is for nature or creature

Love is selfless, love is in kindness,
Love is madness, love is in helpfulness

Love is here, there and everywhere
Just need to felt there and to take care

Love is giving and gaining
Sometimes, Sacrificing …

Love is within you,
Don't be shy to love you
Love is that essence Which spread everywhere,
Just like the air
Love yourself, Love others
It is the Universal language understandable by all of us.

36
An Uninvited Love
Syed Saba Rizvi, Jamia Millia Islamia, New Delhi

So you are coming...that is what doctor told me.
I did not smile, was stricken with fear anxiety and loss of me.
I knew you loved me and I hated you not.
But my aims and dreams had stronger knot
In each passing day you loved me more and wanted more of me.
But I was more into me and myself.

I couldn't sleep for nights and days were tiring,
Evenings were dry and night so scary.
As the days came nearer. I become so far from life
Feeling sick, superlatively frustrated, mood swings killed my
vibes.
You loved me always, I knew it well.
But my dreams and aims had stronger knot.

The moment arrived and I was looking at things oblivious of
anything.
Mind musing but body in deep slumber.
And suddenly you emerged.
Not quietly….not at all.
But your scream wasn't unfriendly to the excruciating pain of
mine..
It seemed a bliss.

But then that was me to answer..
Why questions are seeking answers through me??
I was fixed and watched him in pain and breath,
He came close to me and clung me tightly
I seemed world to him.
He loved me always, I knew it well..

I slyly gazed at him for a moment,
Trying not to align my eye with his eye.
Like a cupid he struck me deep within
And our affair started..

We exchanged rings of relationship
With the promise of eternal bond..

A secret which was unknown was unravelled to me.
He exposed what I masked for so long.
Dreams and aim will have to wait
As he is now my priority straight.
You loved me always I knew it well.
Ma loves you more than ever you would.

37
The Rain
Noor Mohammed Maheera, Auxilium College Vellore

It is a heat
A song of a heart beat
A fever
A running river
A wind whirling, curling tossing
Cursing and mind blowing
A thunder clapping, lighting roof ripping
A feeling, laughing and crying, a gut thwarting
Sweating, throbbing mood toiling
A lion roaring devouring, keeps boiling

What is that?
So charming
Teeth gnawing and stomach churning
Desert sand, a leg in mud sinking
A puzzle can't stop thinking
Music, a samba so blur the rhythm
A poem so nice the rhyming
It's taking yea giving blind confusion
It just understands … a plain confession

Sunshine
Moon light
It's a spot, it feels so right
An angel wings in snow
A heart pudding, face it slow
A candle night of glow
A teacher, it makes you grow
Patience
Conscience
So gentle kind humble it twinkles
A blessing it sprinkles
It is sharing and caring
Healing and curing
A tip

A pit
Fallen in it youngsters merry
And adults marry
An old king and his sages
Council from the rages
It makes elderly behaves chilly
The sane cries silly
Even the beast feast fully

It is a window
A shadow
She's so touched, tip toed and peeping
Mix feeling, deep in the soul he's weeping
What is it?
It's a cloud, shades of love
O bee maker!
Take me to the flower and grain
For love lets together sing "Let it rain".

38
Shades of Love
Aishwarya Lakkakula, RBVRR Women's College, Narayanguda
Hyderabad

I am an Artist
I am in Love
I paint my love
In beautiful Hues and Shades

I wonder!
What is the colour of Love?

I paint my love in some shades of Hearty Blue..
To know my love is Purely True

I paint my love in some shades of Prosperous Green..
To prove my love is Infinitely Ever-Green

I paint my love in some shades of Ruby Pink..
To Letter my love in lovely Ink

I paint my love in some shades of Sharp Yellow..
To pain my love in Sweet Mellow

I paint my love in some shades of pure White..
To cool my love in Snow-White

I paint my love in some shades of Hot Red..
To sleep my love in Rosy Bed

I paint my love in some shades of Baby Brown..
To pride my love in Diamond Crown

I paint my love in some shades of the Darkest Grey..
To fade my love in the Gravest Day

I paint my love in some shades of Star Black..
To promise my love is never taken Aback!

Shades are Bright..Shades are Light...
Shades are Just..Shades are Dust...
But..
My Love is not complete..
Without my "Shades of Love" in it!

39
Shades of Love
Hemasreelatha M, Shri Shankarlal Sundarbai Shasun Jain
College (W) Chennai

He sat near the window with a carton in his hand,
It was the last carton to be taken out of the house.
"Carla's" was written on the top, in bold letters just like her.
His lips were trembling not out of fear or cold
But out of love and sorrow,

-The unexpected and the interminable sorrow.
He wanted to recap all those endearing times with her,
But was afraid as it will increase the depth of the
pit that he had fallen into.
It's been a month ever since she's gone,
gone into nothingness, gone forever.
And this span aided him in identifying the possessor of his true
love.
Was it the girl whom he saw in his 8th birthday party
or was it the girl whom he proposed at 18.
Was it the girl with whom he was in a live- in
or was it the girl for whom he accepted a dark fate.

He and Carla struggled for 5 long years,
She half dead physically and he completely dead mentally
But still a thin ray of hope was always striking his heart and all it
said was
"She will be back, your wife will be back soon!"
And all his numerous battles were only for that
purpose! Only for her to rise back.
But the Grey day arrived,
the day when he had to quit the battle,
The day he realized that she's not going come back -
never the same, never that lively and never again!
And all he can do now is just succour her to end the journey with
less distress and pain.

Quitting battles is not the cup of a brave king

But here for him, the situation demanded more than just being
and being practical he accepted for her euthanasia.

From a hell of blood stains, vomits and capsule loads, he
relieved her into peace – eternal peace.
Because he knew that he can live without her but with
their memories… but definitely not with her being brain
dead!
With Carla in his life he experienced not just true love
But also the spectrumic shades of love.
It started with yellow and ended with black.
Two common colours in life but most impacting SHADES OF
LOVE.

40
The Power of Love
S Vijaya Rekha, Sarojini Naidu Vanita Maha Vidyalaya
Nampally

Love makes many things
Love solves many thinks
One shade makes us GOD and the other DOG
Through emotional we become devotional
It colors mother's love
To feel her glow
It colors father's affection
To feel his attention
It colours brother's amity with security
It colours sister's fond with bond
Friends leave enmity for fraternity
Patriots leave life for nation to prove their passion
Infatuation changes into obsession
Admiration changes into tradition
Sympathy tends to service
Apathy ends to grace
Nature's love preserves all reserves
Natural love rends to sacrifices
Universal love stops anarchy
Removing all deficacy
We heal as we feel
Attitude cherish, gratitude flourish

41
Growing in Love
Dimple Nahata, Alipore Road, Kolkata

Experienced a lifetime
In a couple of years
The moment I hit
The puberty lane
I found everything
Strange and insane
In Brain, Body and Bane
I liked everything toxic
And ran away from
Benign and innocuous
Tried to help the mean
And became mean to humble
Humility didn't exist and
Embarrassment didn't effect
Dated the one who
Hit me more than twice
And played the one
Who caressed me uncountable times
Cherished the one who left me
Forgot the one who helped me
Wondering what was it
That I was running behind
I hit maturity when
I declined the best cover
And held the book with
Simple layout and name
They looked at me
As if I was not sane
For someone who runs
Behind what's on trend
I read the book
Felt utter disgust
Not at the book
But at the choices
I made over and over again

The next day
I booked a stay
To pamper the inner self
To grow love for myself
The much needed vacay
Took me to trips
Of What love looked like
And what people showed
All this time.
I saw a mother milking baby
I saw an old couple swinging
I saw teachers being nice
I saw friends standing by side
I saw couple fighting and patching
I saw siblings cover for each other
I saw humanity
And learnt self-love
Is Part of shades of Love.

42
Shades of Love
Piyali Dey, Seshadripuram First Grade College, Bangalore

From a distance of two hundred and sixty miles,
A call reaches him every single day,
The worry of his mother, if he had food.
The other day, at a toy shop, the five year old
did lift the car for himself, but also
carried a little doll for his two year old sister.
Behind my window pane, a pigeon sits all day long
to safeguard her little ones who feel
warm under their mother's wings.

The sixth grade boy makes sure to carry another
school bag everyday, the bag of his
handicapped friend who smiles at this gesture.
After a long and tiring day at the field,
when the farmer rests down, the tree above,
provides shade, with her leaves, lovingly.
While the soldier remains busy, working for
the country, his wife counts every minute
and waits for his return back home.

The teacher who scolds her student a day
before exam, is the same person who pats his back
when he outshines with flying colors.
Those street vendors who engage in a gossip every day,
Transform into a backbone for
each other, when left in dismay.
Out of concern, the old lady scolds her husband
every single time, when he doesn't
take his medicines, on time.

The seventy-year-old man, residing in the
third floor of the building, expresses his fury
when the cricket ball hits his window
But also, misses the children on days
when they don't come to play.

After a heavy break down, when she's comforted
with a warm hug from her friend, her worries
disappear and her heart gets lighter.

In the evening, when he makes the perfect cup
of tea and hands it over to her, a bright smile
appears on her face, after a day of
juggling between office and house work.
Without uttering a single word, the two share
long silences, not the awkward types
but the happy and comfortable ones.
The ice cream parlor owner, recognizes that
old student even after years, because
he would rush to this place after a hard day at school,
just to lick the chocolate bar and shed his tears.

These few out of the many instances
make me believe in trust and love,
five fingers of the hand aren't the same
but together they make a powerful army,
the most essential part of the body. In the same way,
these shades differ, but are stitched together
with the only precious emotion 'love'.
So different, yet so sweet and pure
That's how I fathom, my dear,
These astounding "shades of love".

43
Shades of Love
Foram Rikky Shah, Shri Shankarlal Sundarbai Shasun Jain
College for Women

A heart that feels, a heart that kills,
The goodness of the soul, the burning of desire.
Oh wanderlust of love, perish and die!
Or I shall hang! your love, my demise!

One I see, the younger me,
The love of innocence that spreads.
The fairytale of dreams, oh that fairytale!
A fairytale that slowly shreds.

Demons inside of love that holds,
The jealousy of Aphrodite that kills!
My innocence not beauty, I put to the Gods,
Oh, but demons possess what? I am at his will.

I hope it all be fine, drunk with a glass of wine,
All fears flow, all tears cry! My heart broke,
My heart heals, my heart broke, my heart heals,
A wanderlust of love it is, I am fine.

Darkness in my soul, fire in my heart,
A wound that holds, a hope of spark.
I see him there, the devil and his dance,
Fire! Fire! Let me be yours!

The shades of love, polluted by lust,
Love never found me, I never found love.
I knew love hurts, but I never loved.
Oh, the only love I know, is dead.

There was no one to love, no one to care,
No one to see, for as far as I could see.
Narcissus was a divine right, for what love I seek,
Love I find in me and all other's dead?

I saw it all, it burns in monotonous tasks.
I'm tired and soulless and I finally found love.
There he stands before me, brave and tall.
Oh, come to me, my beloved death, my love!

My true love, come at last!
Riding on the black steed, looking all smart.
My heartbeat fades, the heart finally stops.
The only true love, that waited, O I have finally come!

My child! My child! Come back to me! She cried.
Oh mother dearest, I could, if only I was alive.
She loved me too, too dearly to see,
Forgive me, mother, I was blinded by my agony.

I had hoped, I would be saved, I had hoped
To found love. I didn't, my heart broke,
I wept for him, and he laughed.
The shades of love fading away, blood pouring.

I killed him, I did. He laughed and stopped.
I saw fire and the devil in him, I killed him.
My fairytale ruined, my heartbroken,
A love of madness, a kiss to his heart, I did.

I loved him, alive and dead, for his soul
still ugly of his sins! I pulled him close,
his lifeless soul, Oh his pale lips I kissed.
I looked at his heart that bled, a knife within.

Tragic lovers, they'll say. Romeo and Juliet,
they'll call us. But, nay, he loved me not,
Nor any love left in me. But, he died because of me,
And I for him and we'll be remembered for our tragic love story!

That'll serve his soul! Punish him to demise!
My love that bled, my love shall rise! He
loves me not, but every one shall think he did,
What more punishment can I serve his soul, than love?

44
Shades of Love
Razanna Niaz, Mosque Street, Madhavalayam, Kanyakumari

Million shades of love
Merging the living
Mesmerizing the magical
Thoughts of life!
Ambitious ardent love
Beloved betrothed love
Comforting caressing love
Desirous delicate love
Ecstatic eternal love
Fantastic friendly love
Genuine growth love
Hectic hilarious love
Ingenuous immortal love
Joyous jingling love
Kind keen love
Loyal long awaited love
Magnanimous magnificent love
Noble nectar love
Obeisant original love
Precious paramount love
Questing quality love
Radiant rainbow love
Soothing sensual love
Tender thoughtful love
Unconditional unique love
Valid varied love
Worthy wowed love
Xenial xerophytic love
Yielding yearning love
Zestful zingy love –
All brushed in bouquet
Of my love by mighty master
Adding colours to my span
Each stroke leaving a
Lasting impression

In the pages of my mortal life
Magically weaving with
My immortal life!!
Blessed is me to
feel the fathom of love
intertwined in my brocade
garmented with brooches
of righteous deeds
ultimately destining me to
your kingdom of heaven!!!

45
I love you like this
Muskan Jain, Amity University Madhya Pradesh

PEOPLE WILL WANT YOU IN THEIR LIFE,
BUT I UNDERSTAND YOU IN MY LIFE,
I LOVE YOU LIKE THIS

PEOPLE WILL PRAY TO ACHIEVE YOU,
BUT I PRAY FOR YOU
I LOVE YOU LIKE THIS

MILLIONS WOULD LIKE TO LIVE WITH YOU,
BUT I WANT TO DIE WITH YOU
I LOVE YOU LIKE THIS

ALL YOUR MISTAKES TELL YOU,
I WANT TO BE THE REASON FOR CORRECTING YOUR MISTAKES
I LOVE YOU LIKE THIS

I DO EVERYTHING IN MY HEART WITHOUT FEAR,
YOU KNOW HOW MUCH I AM AFRAID OF LOSING YOU
I LOVE YOU LIKE THIS

YOU THINK WE DO NOT CARE ABOUT YOU,
BUT WHAT DO YOU KNOW YOU RECOGNIZE US,
TELL ME HOW MUCH I DIE ON YOU
I LOVE YOU LIKE THIS

HOW CAN I TELL YOU WHAT YOU DO,
I START WITH YOU ALL MY MORNING,
I CAN'T EVEN LIVE WITHOUT TALKING TO YOU
I LOVE YOU LIKE THIS

WE DON'T MAKE EVERYONE OUR FRIEND,
'KASHISH' IS UNIQUE AMONG YOU,
YOU TAKE MY MIND WITHOUT SAYING,
YOU HAVE LEARNED THIS ART FROM
YOU KNOW, I DON'T KNOW HOW TO SHOW CONCERN,

I COULD NEVER EXPRESS MY FEELINGS FOR YOU
BUT BELIEVE ME, YOU ARE VERY SPECIAL TO ME
VERY CLOSE TO MY HEART
I LOVE YOU LIKE THIS

THE HEART TRIES TO TALK TO YOU DAY AND NIGHT, BUT I AM
AFRAID THAT I WILL NOT LOSE YOU LIKE EVERYONE ELSE
YOU ARE LIKE MY FAMILY IN MY FRIEND, YOU ARE THE
SWEETEST ASPECT OF MY LIFE
I LOVE YOU LIKE THIS.

46
Zodiac Love
Abhijit Seal, Cotton University, Panbazar, Guwahati, Assam

An Aries will chase passionately after the deer
long till the other half comes near
A Taurus rides a bull in traditional heart
with toughness stand still right from the start
A Gemini is dual in every way still
and loves the one who communicates words and feel
A Cancer shall stick grounded till the end
no hanky-pranky business when heart is lend
A Leo leads the pack like a leader in a crowd
showering warmth and comfort to beloved in proud
A Virgo opens heart with precision and grace
like neatness follows a bride of taste
A Libra delves purely with sweet heart's glove
and balances scale akin love is life
A Scorpio is possessive and strategically progressed
and in build a home with love of the suitor's nest
A Sagittarius runs wild that the mind thinks
to discover a firm route in lover's link
A Capricorn is rigid and longs love like a timber
when leads ambition to reach top with labour
An Aquarius is wind in every corner
but the true feelings preserve heart for the lover
A Pisces receives a bit of luck from the divine graced
in searching a soul mate bond in spiritual paces.
Now, they are far more than my words can trace
know not I of every soul, but a little I can
and so does their feelings oozes in Valentine's face
till love find its place
in the heart of human race.

47

Divine Love
Jyoti Kushwaha, Bundelkhand University, Jhansi

Blessed are those who know,
What it is to love and what it is to be loved....

In the journey of life, LOVE,
Is experienced in many forms,
And expressed in many hues,
Difficult to define, unique in feeling,
Relationships give love different shades and meaning.

With relatives, colleagues and friends,
I experienced CONDITIONAL LOVE which lasted,
Till I could attend, pretend and spend.

With mother, I discovered love is UNCONDITIONAL,
For a mother's heart is never her own,
Bits of it are sown into her children born.

Conditional love has conditions applied,
Unconditional love lasts till the giver is in life,
But love that is beyond time, conditions and being,
Is the DIVINE LOVE that will stay forever with me.
All may go and all may leave,
But my Lord will never forsake me!!

48
Find Love Around
Khubi Ram, Aggarwal Public School, Ballabgarh

Love, on earth, has innumerable shades -
Ever seen a rustic who a shallow river wades.

Love now dances on the petals of a flower,
Then it sings on the twigs of the spring.

Trembles in the caring eyes of a 'mom',
Also sleeps quietly in the walls of a dome.

Love is love and knows other emotions none,
Found in plenty in the lines of Keats and Donne.

Thrilling art is love, as pure as raindrops,
Blooming of flowers in winter as one hopes.

What cuckoo and nightingale sings - is love,
What nature whispers in life's ears - is love.

True love is rare - but say- liveth where?
One should go to find - in a club or a fair.

Love is sweet; as well may be sour,
Don't judge rain by dust with, it may pour.

Love dwells on the pink lips of a sweet 'love',
May assure you in the pure snow of a 'dove'.

Love is blue sky; and love is earth brown,
Softer than a tear and stronger than a crown.

Love is as wise as a father's strict counsel,
And is same precious as a mother's.

Love is butterfly, sucking nector from 'leaves',
Love is 'simple sheep' in stable as one sees.

Love is when mind doesn't play a part,
Pure heart is there, silent without a word.

Love means 'sighs' rising from the deep,
It is proven if one without reason weep.

Love is beheld in the blue eyes of the beloved,
Seen in the quiet laugh of as said aboved.

Love is immortal, and never does it die,
Will know if you live 'love' - don't ask why?

Love is what a spouse seeks in you,
Don't need a word, just look, watch and woo.

Love is not but a sacrifice, with reasons none,
It's a 'smooth nod' when father deals with his son.

Love with 'care' isn't and can't be a true form,
It's gods' blessings which knows no norm.

Love is truth, love is life and 'giving' for all,
Love is duty, love is beauty and is life's call.

When a bee makes honey, love happens,
It plays its part when peace comes but no weapons.

Love is the beginning, love is the end,
The rest are mere blue, dew, air, heat and sand.

49
Shades of Love
Rathod Hetal, Krantiguru Shyamji Krushna Verma Kachchh
University, Bhuj

Love has its own shades,
When hearts tie a knot
And eyes find its light.
The Sea sings melodious quote
And the sky shines in a night
Then love illuminates in a life.

It has power to own things
Too has fragility of fear to lose.
When it comes with all its power
It can turn war into peace
And a curse becomes boon,
Then love makes its own light.

Love beautifully makes pair
When care becomes cure,
The people could be fake
But true love always remain pure.
The world could be demised
But the love will continue to survive.

Nothing can bind its blaze
Because it gives wing to freedom.
It has everything to turn border into heaven.
So, colour doesn't matter in its kingdom.
Love has many shades to create charm
Because it is connected by hearts.

50
Colour Zone
Aashi Prasad, Jyoti Nivas College, Bangalore

It was thou forth love
Which made the pain unbearable
And the words heard
Stung like needles
Brilliant crimson turned to faded black
Love once cherished
Turned into tortured wrath
Sense of self forgotten
Self harm will always turn a flower rotten

Beginnings were filled with shades of pink
Sweet shy hopeful love
Asked for blessings from the moon
Phase of trials to become
Someone perfect with qualities hiding
Your imperfections
Becomes a daily routine
Whispering yet soundless duvets of Red
Starts engorging itself into hopeful love
To give rise to brilliant crimson

Crimson the colour of Passion
Burned the flames
Significant to powerful love
This love which sprouted soaring wings
Created a strong mindset to move forth
Happiness at it's peak
Even chrysanthemums bloomed red
A mirage of fairy tail created
Prevented self from seeing white engulfing red
Sparks to disappear
And hollowness to prevail
Dreams were finally shattered by a cleft
Wings disappeared
Red disappeared

Leaving nothing but stark white

Reality came back to life
It's claws cutting away the fairy tail
White surrounded the mind
White gave options
Start or revert back
White morphed into black
When blackness soared
Ashes rained down from the sky
Emptiness befell
Droplets of years of pain finally bled Maroon
It made one realise
That all this time the shades of colour
Blending through the heart was of unrequited love

Heart broken, blacked out
But a speck of white still alive
Time started
White blended with black
To give grey
Grey pushed and pushed
Till the entire heart engulfed
Painful experience gave lesson
Happiness gave strength
Combining both grey gave the heart
Self-love
With flaws accepted,
Imperfections turned over to beauty marks
Love burning for another
Started burning for oneself
Person finally bloomed
Shining like a star

51
The Broken Heart
Mamidi Shireesha, Andhra University, Vishakapatnam

Oh my stupid heart! Stop craving for love,
You can't weigh it's depth at any cost.
You rather consult the broken heart,
Who had experienced the whole of love.

Come, go through the lane of memories.
Began with million hopes towards love,
Ending with billion pieces of broken heart,
Dying every second inside those tiny pieces.

Then, when on clouds nine, flourished with belief.
Now, when painted with autumn greyness,
Fainted with fear of holding faith in any colour,
Being lost in the darkness of detrimental love.

Doubt not, you never meet certainty,
Cause love itself is uncertain, my dear.
Yes!! It's the most baleful one ever
It has many shades within...

52
Shades of Love
Ahalya, Pandaravilai, Kandanvilai, Kanyakumari

A beautiful painting is the result of different shades of colour
A beautiful life is the result of different shades of love
Mother's love is the caring shade
Represents the purity of milk
Father's love is the protecting shade
Represents the sacrificing heart of pelican
Love of the siblings is the sweet and naughty shade
Represents the innocence of the new born baby
Our better half's love is unconditional and eternal shade
Represents the blood in every veins
A friend's love is the helping shade
Represents the bliss of the flourished greens
Pure shades of love... Feel it, enjoy it and adhere it to the core
Every helping hands represents a shade of love
Every hand that embraces you represents a shade of love
Light or dark or cool or warm every shades of love are precious
to every heart
Love is infinity... the characteristic of God
Only God is aware of all the shades of love
Enjoy every shade of love God showers on you.
Never be possessive with Love
Share the shades of love with others
Encounter new shades of love every day
Let life prosper every second with the shades of love.

53
Shades of Love

Upanisha S, Avinashilingam Institute for HS & HE for Women
Coimbatore

The heat of passion alone does not importance to love denote,
Meek love can withstand the test of time as well.
The love of a man does his character display.
The meek love meekly, while the strong love strong.
Often however, time does favour the patience of the meek.
And when the death knell tolls, all shades of love will their glory
find.

54
The Rainbow
Vishnu Priya J, Bharathamatha College of Arts and Sciences
Kozhnjampara

When you care for me,
You're my best friend.
When you love me;
You change as my half boy friend.
When you protect me,
You seemed like my brother.
When you avoid me;
Then you are my enemy.
When you understand my feelings;
You are my soulmate.

At last I realised
Friendship shares lots of love
You're my rainbow:
Who share different shades of love.
It's you; you're my shade of love,
It's you my friend.

55
Shades of Love
Jyotsana, Mata Sundari College for Women, Delhi

When in ninth, your grandpa held me tight.
Kissed at the sight, your grandpa told me the right,

From marriage to holding to carriage,
We did it together, hold our hands forever,

The reality and beauty we hold,
In hard times necklaces we sold,

From education to parable telling,
He built confidence inside me,

The grandma you see today,
Is the beauty of your grandma inside me,

He stared, I blushed,
He kissed, I cuddled,

We convinced our parents,
Enounced the lovely life,

From tureen to open,
From ice scoops to try,

we two are shades of love, no lies no hides.

56
Shades of Love
Mickey Manaswini, Balugaon, Khordha

Never in someone's warm arms
Forever to be someone's princess
How it feels
Is every girl's zeal.

But being dark
With full of pimple
Considered a jerk
Love degraded to surreal

Beauty lies not in the eyes of beholder
Defined in the fairness of the seducer
Give me one instance of true love
Where love survives bodily crave.

Nothing is true
True means eternal
When we r ephemeral
It just spills a new hue

Many are taken to the crimson glow
Many lose there identity with the flow
It is the dice of the one
Who can genuinely feign

Love
When felt feels like fantasy come true;
When shared should make us feel good;
It never goes away when it is well defined;
It is truly said that beyond cast colour n creed;
If You are jealous weaker gets the thread
Which accommodates everyone in only garland

That's a little in the variety of shades of love
Which is another word next to peace n dove.

57
The Moonlight
Dhanashree Das, Indira Gandhi National Open University
Guwahati

The bed was warm and fine,
I put my head on the pillow
That wore a lavish silk colour on it.
The outside was a little cold but
Its whispering sound
Told me the spring was in delight.
The swinging of my mind,
The delicate nerves of my body,
The sound of the heartbeat
Went to the place
Where your presence existed.
The moonlight shone through
The skinny white clouds,
Taking my eyes to the ground
Where the moonlight was taking rest and sit,
The moonlight was you
And the dust coming through
The broken glass of the window was me,
Still, we were together,
Stayed with each other.

58
The Bearded Man's Funeral
Anagha Agnes, Pondicherry University

Miles apart, beyond the Prussian blue ocean
Resides my bearded man
In his 70s, resting his spine on an armchair
Contemplating the melancholic rain and
Sipping his vintage lemon tea,
And I am melting in this distance.
It was always a terse summer or a fleeting winter.
Now, Should I lament for my early goodbyes?
I am counting the trees flashing by on my rear mirror
Maybe to betray the ticking clock.

Today, I realize that I am the cursed daughter.
Like an adrift sailor, I stand still
Witnessing his cold feet tied up in white
It is my curse that you are departing in this pandemic.
With fear and fury, the natives rebuked,
And I still longed for a glimpse of his face.
But the curse was resolute, and the natives were numb.
I saw the Priest with his cross pointed at me
I was the threat, the beholder of the virus.
As a stranger, I saw a white-cloaked body taken away,
And my mother and brother accompanying a procession.
Like a terrifying tale, all was said and done.
The tale of the bearded man's funeral
Where his cursed daughter was banished.

59
The Snake's Love
Sooraj Lal SB, Tattamangalam, Palakkad

There was this snake,
Who loved a rose.
His love was something
Beyond normality.

There was this snake,
Silent and enigmatic.
Whereas his love symbolized
Tranquility and winsomeness.

There was this snake,
Who knew his love
Was harmful as the thorns
Which protected her could kill him.

There was this snake,
Who coiled around
His beloved rose.
Only to detriment himself.

There was this snake,
Who met his end as
Gluttony played its mind games
And love gave its directions.

There was this snake,
Who lived in a society,
Where love was a dichotomized
Entity and much more detrimental.

There was this snake,
Who died of agony,
As he loved someone
Not of his kind.

60
Shades of Love
Achudha S, St Joseph's College of Arts and Science, Cuddalore
Tamil Nadu

After a long wait …
I found, all in one.
A caring Mom,
A protecting Dad,
A sharing Sister,
A supporting Brother,
An eternal Friend,
An inspiring Skylark,
A singing Nightingale,
A horrifying Thunder,
An arguing Portia,
A humble Cordelia,
An optimizing Westwind,
An unsolvable Mystery,
An enlightening Book,
An exhilarating Pain,
A torturing Dude,
A twinkling Star,
A flourishing Flood,
Who is He?
LOVE.
His shades are numerous,
Who makes the life luminous.

61
Reminder to Sweetheart
Rachit Dave, Odhav Avenue, Pramukhswami Nagar Bhuj

Red flower and rosy, valentine day and cosy
Writing this love letter, feel always friendly
Dark light, you fear, but Keep you intact dear
Titled shades of love, so shed tears never tear
Remember first sight, how reached the height
Love, dreams at night, knight bright path right
Garland in my hand, sweet songs with band
Oh love! day dreaming, wishing hand in hand
Petty memories pretty, pangs of love tolerably
Withstand with love, shades of sorrow lovingly
Rainbow shedding colour, earth filled odour
Darling! plant sapling, shades of love nurture
Posting peace of mind, the matter never mind
The true love is the truth, It prevails I remind

62
Shades of Love
D Ruban Prabu, Kovilpatti, Thoothukudi

You never have a shape,
Whereas your absence is nowhere,
You producing penchant, causing compassion,
Makes everyone go forward.

Love – an ineffable thing,
Abstract, abundant, sometimes agonizing,
You reign over the creature,
Being entwined with you.

You remind me of all I adore,
Evoking the care of my mother,
Bringing out the tears she shed;
All that provoked her care for me is You- Love.

You push the heartless inwardly,
To have pity on the helpless kindly.
The most powerful one you are,
Being reckoned as the equivalence of God.

You, mother of humanity and unity,
Be cultivated in every human being,
To make us unbiased, helpful,
To give you a visible body.

63
Shades of Love
CS Ashitha Hanna, East Peruvilai, Nagercoil

Love is universal,
Lots of love scattered among the narrow world,
Its beyond race, racism, wealth and power,
It transfers through smile, help and care,
from a stranger or someone else,
And the bliss will follow till the entire life,
Even in the dark and in the light it couldn't fade,
And the sparks glitters throughout the end,
Human will fade but the shades of love will always remain.

64
Incomplete but Unconditional Love
Prakruti Vinayak Naik, Om Sai Dham, Davangere

I know, I could not be yours,
For if I could have, peace would have resided in heart of ours.
Nevertheless, as I see you now,
My hands get lifted and how.
Praying for your eternal happiness,
Although there will always be some emptiness….

Whoever shall enter in your life,
As your newly wedded wife.
Shall love you a little more than I did,
Fight little less than we did.
Stand by you in all odds & against all odds,
Because she is sent to you from the gods….

When your heart will become full with love from her,
My empty heart will reach out to you in a whisper.
As love may not always end when apart,
It will always bloom for you in my heart.
So, I pray your life blossoms without any thorn of my
incomplete love,
But with lots and lots of Unconditional Love.

65
To Love is to Live!
Ayesha Rahman, Lucknow

A little contented, a little forlorn,
She watched quietly as it rained,
She remembered vividly how the rains made her dance,
She remembered vividly how he swung her around,
She remembered vividly how he dried her wet locks in a frenzy
with his svelte fingers,
She remembered vividly because..
She knew to remember was to relive!

A little contented, a little forlorn,
She remembered vividly how their conversations merged into an
ocean of comfortable silence,
She remembered vividly how they watched intently as the pitter
and patter would come to an end and the sky would shine clean
and bright again,
She remembered vividly how he arrived one evening amidst the
stormy rains wrapped in white,
She remembered vividly how her wet locks did not dry that
evening...because his svelte fingers could not reach them!
She remembered vividly because..
She knew to remember was to relive!

A little contented, a little forlorn,
She remembered vividly that no matter it was shortlived..yet she
had received intense love once!
She remembered vividly that even though he was gone...she still
felt his presence in absence!
She remembered vividly that to love once meant to love always
and forever!
She remembered vividly that to love in itself was to revive one's
own heart!
She remembered vividly because...
She knew to remember was to relive!!

66
Love is Divine
Tanya Tripathi, IFHE, Donthanpalle, Telangana

My heart says it in a silent voice,
As my trembling heart blooms with rejoice.
In this living world of pricing cries,
You planted seed of dreams in my eyes.
I will be your magical sword and strongest shield,
And will always stand next to you in battlefield.
In inky sea of thundering storms and wandering wave,
You are the guiding wind that made me brave.
My agonizing scars breaths countless secrets of mine,
And yet you say my broken heart will always shine.
My tears were hugged by your fingers of hopes,
As you unleashed me from old suffocating ropes.
In the drowning hours of deep lonely night,
You are the celestial bliss of enchanting light.
Our souls were blessed with a feeling greater than love,
As our fates bounded by strings of destiny from above.

67
Paint My Skies Happy
Bishal Bimal Mazumdar, Nalbari College, Nalbari, Assam

I'm looking into the dark of the night, sleepless
I've been searching for you, but it's so cold,
The world feels empty, my heart's a mess
I'm standing in front of a mirror, being ever so bold.
We're a people with crushed dreams and broken mirrors,
We make up a facade, to hide our breaths of errors.
I've been looking, never knowing what for,
Pleasure of the heart? My internal war.
Maybe you are just a journey,
In my delirium, a pursuit mistaken,
An infinite pavement for me to follow
This hideous winter, acting as my therapy,
Someday if you decide to visit me,
I'll be painting my skies happy.

68
The Heart Weeps to Smile
Tabinda Naiyer, Bardhaman

Even the word cruel is shy
tears trickled down my cheeks as I cry
cruel is my fate - my very own
that deceived
NO MERCY SHOWN!!
The small happiness,
someone to adore, is what I begged for.
It plucked the rose that blossomed in my heart
left behind was its thorn in my part.
The thorn pierced my heart again and again
till it injured its every part.
It shattered into pieces
and indeed it hurts
still not a word said, the heart got torn apart.
So many hurdles to cross
seven seas across,
What a condition of mine
not happiness but
SORROWS ON CLOUD NINE!!

69
Intertwined Love
Tayyaba Barqi, Amity University Dubai

I had absorbed your love in my heart
How soil absorbs water
I felt your love deep inside me
like my veins getting watered every day

You'd come to me every morning
And be the ray of sun for my heart
And in return my heart would turn into a flower bed

Your love was just like my flowers
Deeply rooted inside my heart
Plucking any one of them would cause me damage and diminish
my beauty

Every day my flowers turned more beautiful
And you kept wondering the secret behind it
It has always been you and
My love for you will never cease to exist
For I have intertwined the roots of my flowers
With the roots of your love.

70
Reminiscence
Nandhini A, Lady Doak College, Madurai

Wind chime swings,
Clunking and clanging in the gust.
Sky as blue as my life
Succumbs to the dark clouds,
Like I to his memories.
Lingers my feeling like the floral scent of red wax chunks,
He put in the warmer years back.
The serene room fills loneliness in my void heart.
Craving for his care,
I sigh in the humid air.
Screaming a silent scream,
Slate-blue eyes well up with tears
And whirl within the Ornate frame on livid wall.
I gaze, not the Eiffel Tower drenched in frost
Or snow drops soliciting dust,
Neither his black jerkin nor his blue torn jean,
But his beady brown eyes hid partly in shades.
Drowning in the surging sea of thoughts,
I envy the air fondling his hair.
The portrait seems alive,
Along with the moments we met
And the seconds we fell in love,
Still fresh as the maiden beam of Sun.
Tears roll down on my cheeks
Widen the ocean in between us,
Yet his love shines through my pale life
Like scarlet salvias scattered on ice.

71
Nature has its own Shades of Love-2
Atiendriya Verma, VIT University, Bhopal, Madhya Pradesh

Some Where Shine and shade have their sack race
Somewhere Tree and Traveler have them prorogue
Somewhere clouds and birds surpass
Somewhere sea is cease for her adorable river
Nature has its own shades of love-2
Somewhere barren land has thirsty eyes for cloud
Somewhere swirl dance for emerging petal
Somewhere ocean of sea fall for mirage
Somewhere marsh soil and lotus are in different relation
Nature has its own shades of love-2
Somewhere air and rain are in aroma
Somewhere land and cloud are in allure
Somewhere sun and sunflower make confession
Somewhere moon and Crepe Jasmine have deep love silence
Nature has its own shades of love-2
Somewhere sand is making earth artistic
Somewhere peacock dance refines the beauty of rain
Somewhere shell and pearls promise to live together
Somewhere night and star are coverage their love
Nature has its own shades of love-2

72
Words to Paint You

Surya Ratna Sarvani Addanki, Dr Sarvepalli Radhakrishna Arts
College Visakhapatnam

Somedays I search for words
Among the waters and the woods
To paint you, my marvel
Who was my fortune of time travel
I wandered among these whites and blues
I wish to collect their lovely hues
Those hues of nebulas
Portrayed your warm love as circles
I rushed along the rivers of life
And found your essence of love of rife
I swam across the Milky Way
And found the light of your eyes all the way
The crescent, that curvy one
It resembled your smile,
The precious one
And the ambered rays
Remembered the warmth of lullaby, in slumber
I searched for words
But I found wonders
Of life and universe
Through your soul and your mind
I wish to paint you my marvel
With hues of my love
As You filled the cosmos
With you
And also me
Let me paint and smile
For the one last time forever
And let me lay down
Peacefully in my eternity

73
Shades of Love
Lorna Barbara Erla, Jagran Lakecity University, Mugaliyachap
Bhopal (MP)

These wonderful Diwali sights,
Bathe shades of love
In shades of light.

Violet, pink, green or red,
And curtains of twinkling gold,
Children tucked cozy into bed,
Couples escaping for a midnight stroll.
As the diligent friend sees his charge home,
Such is the diligent flame flickering in breeze,
A patient scholar illuminates each tome,
A kaleidoscope of light as far as an eye can see.
And just like the homes squeezed side by side,
Is the closeness of each human soul,
Reflects the kinship we feel inside,
No matter what media shows.

Illuminate people on all days,
In the shades of love,
And lead the way.

74
A Lot like Love
S Nandhini, The American College, Madurai

They say love comes in all shades;
Agape, Philia, Eros and Storge.
Fancy words that drops like a grenade.
With care, passion and lust forged,
Some are healthy, some are not.
Let's be honest, I have loved a lot.

I was fifteen and I was in love
Or so I thought but that's not the point.
I was in love and I still wonder how
Everything just fell disjoint.
Promises broken, tears shed,
Letters Burned and heart bled.

I was twenty and I was in love
Or so I thought but that's not the point.
In the world of flings and date,
Our love was like the turtledove.
But that's the funny thing about fate.
Circumstances blamed, hearts deflate.

I was twenty five and I was in love
Or so I thought but that's not the point.
Promises were made, rings exchanged.
Oh boy, do happily ever after even exist?
Hearts turned; only constant is change.
Hands raised and separate we go.

They say love comes in all shades;
Agape, Philia, Eros and Storge.
Fancy words that drops like a grenade.
With care, passion and lust forged,
Some are healthy, some are not.
Let's be honest, I'm done with the lot.

75
Definitions of Love
Shruti Ganesh, National Institute of Design, Ahmedabad

Everywhere you read they say
Love is the colour red.
Like fire.
Like blood.
With equal amounts of passion and pain.
Love is burning in such a pleasure
Where you covet and own and possess
And like a wild instinct
Hold on to skin, to bones, and to memories.

Everywhere he wrote he would say
Love isn't red.
At least, not just that itself.
It is a spectrum beyond what our mere words
Or bare understanding of chemical interactions
Can even begin to define.

They say you are a lover
If you know the taste of kiss bruised lips
Know of the scent of skin and hair, trembling
Of a burning passion beyond metaphors

He never negated that, but his love encompasses more.
His definition of love, wrote he,
Would never be devoid of the warmth of the morning sun
Of softly exchanged glances and touches beyond veils
Of the scent and sensation
Of everything from skin to hair to fur.
To the overwhelming bubbling emotion beyond need in your
heart
A warm gentle feeling settling in the depths of your being
Like a gentle breeze on a hot day.

He wrote it was the effort
He made to befriend the neighbourhood cat

And the softness of its fur as it nuzzled closer.
He wrote of letters on old papers
Passed from friend to friend.
Folded in repetitive lines-
A fragment, a plane, a boat.
He wrote about learning to play the guitar
Of singing under the stars for the first time and not being teased
Of the liquid warmth of a genuine smile
Of the smell of firewood on a colder night.
Of family, both blood bound and found.
Of wrinkles over old skin, and laugh lines around gentle eyes.

And the more he wrote the more he was stumped
By people who refused to accept his words.
It's written pretty, they said.
But that is not love.
It's not love. No it is not.
And though spun well the song he had sung
They didn't acknowledge it in the end.

But maybe the words he should have received
Those he deserved to hear,
Should have been about the beauty of the love he defined.
It's grace, it's lovely design.

I wonder how to convey it.
These words I want to share
Brought about by words of a man alive centuries ago
Who seems to have shared a similar heart as my own...
I know not how to say them after all.

76
The Red Friend
Garima Nandal, Sonipat, Haryana

Unalloyed love seek a quest
Affordable baggage awaits smile

To mitigate all the salt from that pillow
Salt of a taker
Camouflaged as a friend

Crowd was eager to know
The reason behind all

Hidden behind that smile
What can I say
It all commenced with
That trivial poky scratch
In the mirror
Or just an excuse?
Only she knows

Division of will
Smashed mirror of memories
And a glass-path awaited

77
Shades of Love
Abdu Rahiman M, Kolathur, Malappuram, Kerala

Love is pure;
It can make Romeos and Juliets
Sacrifice their lives
On its altar.

Sweet as honey, pure as dew,
Love has untouched only a few.

Love is strong;
It can crystalize itself into
Gigantic Tajmahals.

Strong as a deserted lover's vengeance
Still sweet as wild jasmin's fragrance.

Love is beautiful;
Yeah, but to a lover
His love's object is most beautiful.

Love can beautify a savage's heart
Oh! love, where in history you haven't played a part?

And love is blind;
Love made Roman kings forget their duty
They saw only the Egyptian queen's beauty.

Love is blind, love is kind
It contains the essence of human kind.

But love is flexible;
Yes dear, love is also very flexible
Or tell me why
The lover who saw greener pastures
Told his lover
"My love to you is as a brother's"?

To some, love is measurable in terms of money
Alas! love, glorified by poets many.
Yet you will go on gluing the world
Sung and praised by people like a bird!

78
To the Love of Lifetimes
Niteesh KR, Nagasandra, Bangalore

You might ask what's the occasion.
With you, every day is a celebration.
Who would have thought Snapchat could be a place
Where I will meet my soul mate,
The one I want to spend millions of years with and brought
together by fate.

You are the most beautiful, amazing, pretty, lovely person
anyone will ever come across,
Every time I see you, my heart skips a beat and my life has a
pause.
I was never like this, you bring out the best version,
It is your presence in my life, that makes me the luckiest person.

Meeting you at an early stage has its own perks and benefit,
We walk and grow through every phase together, and sky isn't a
limit.
You are the love of my life, and I have never felt like this before,
You are the only one who matters to me, the one I adore.

Thank you for understanding me so perfectly,
And loving me for who I am, unconditionally.
I wish to spend a lifetime and more with you, it's true,
You are my universe, and I love you.

9 798585 819377